Big Book of NOPE

A private place to be angry, ugly, and totally offensive

By, _____

Copyright © 2016 Dana Kirk
Cover art copyright 2016 Maryna Salagub
All rights reserved.
ISBN-13: 978-0692658123
ISBN-10: 0692658122

A word about this book from school counselor Shelly Roe

I hate writing. I'd so much rather talk about stuff than write about it. But sometimes I can't talk about things. Sometimes I don't want people to hear the things I want to talk about. Sometimes people don't want to listen to the things I have to say, or they don't have time to listen. Sometimes the things I want to say are scary or hurtful or just too sad. And sometimes I'm really happy or excited about something, but I don't want other people to know about it. Then, I write. Then I don't hate writing so much. Then, writing feels good. And I feel good. All my thoughts and feelings can leave my brain and stay on the paper. And later, I can read those thoughts and feelings. Sometimes that's where it ends. But sometimes, I learn something. And then, I start writing again.

So, Reader, maybe you're like me. Maybe you hate writing. Or maybe you love writing. Either way, this book might help you. It definitely can't hurt you. Give it a shot.

Date

Today I am
_____
_____

Because
_____
_____
_____
_____

I wish I could
_____
_____
_____
_____
_____
_____

What I can do is
_____
_____
_____
_____
_____
_____
_____

Date

Today I am

_____
_____

Because

_____
_____
_____
_____

I wish I could

_____
_____
_____
_____
_____

What I can do is

_____
_____
_____
_____
_____
_____

Date

Today I am

_____

_____

Because

_____

_____

_____

_____

I wish I could

_____

_____

_____

_____

_____

What I can do is

_____

_____

_____

_____

_____

_____

_____

Date

Date

Today I am
_____
_____

Because
_____
_____
_____
_____
_____

I wish I could
_____
_____
_____
_____
_____
_____
_____

What I can do is
_____
_____
_____
_____
_____
_____
_____

Date

Today I am

_____
_____

Because

_____
_____
_____
_____

I wish I could

_____
_____
_____
_____
_____

What I can do is

_____
_____
_____
_____
_____
_____
_____

Date

Today I am

_____
_____

Because

_____
_____
_____
_____
_____

I wish I could

_____
_____
_____
_____
_____
_____
_____

What I can do is

_____
_____
_____
_____
_____
_____
_____
_____

Date

Today I am
_____
_____

Because
_____
_____
_____
_____

I wish I could
_____
_____
_____
_____
_____

What I can do is
_____
_____
_____
_____
_____
_____

Date

Today I am

_____
_____

Because

_____
_____
_____
_____
_____

I wish I could

_____
_____
_____
_____
_____
_____
_____

What I can do is

_____
_____
_____
_____
_____
_____
_____

Date

Something that happened today

How I wish it happened

Date

Today I am

_____

_____

Because

_____

_____

_____

_____

I wish I could

_____

_____

_____

_____

_____

_____

What I can do is

_____

_____

_____

_____

_____

_____

_____

Date

Today I am

_____
_____

Because

_____
_____
_____
_____

I wish I could

_____
_____
_____
_____
_____
_____

What I can do is

_____
_____
_____
_____
_____
_____
_____

Date

Today I am
___
___

Because
___
___
___
___
___

I wish I could
___
___
___
___
___
___

What I can do is
___
___
___
___
___
___
___
___

Date

Date

Today I am

_____
_____

Because

_____
_____
_____
_____
_____

I wish I could

_____
_____
_____
_____
_____
_____
_____

What I can do is

_____
_____
_____
_____
_____
_____
_____

Date

Today I am
_____
_____

Because
_____
_____
_____
_____

I wish I could
_____
_____
_____
_____
_____

What I can do is
_____
_____
_____
_____
_____
_____
_____

Date

Today I am

Because

I wish I could

What I can do is

Date

Today I am

_____

_____

Because

_____

_____

_____

_____

I wish I could

_____

_____

_____

_____

_____

What I can do is

_____

_____

_____

_____

_____

_____

_____

Date

Today I am

_____

_____

Because

_____

_____

_____

_____

I wish I could

_____

_____

_____

_____

_____

_____

What I can do is

_____

_____

_____

_____

_____

_____

Date

This SUCKS

Things that Suck	Because	What I can do about it
1.	1.	1.
2.	2.	2.
3.	3.	3.
4.	4.	4.
5.	5.	5.
6.	6.	6.
7.	7.	7.
8.	8.	8.
9.	9.	9.
10.	10.	10.

Date

Today I am

_____

_____

Because

_____

_____

_____

_____

I wish I could

_____

_____

_____

_____

_____

_____

What I can do is

_____

_____

_____

_____

_____

_____

_____

Date

Today I am

Because

I wish I could

What I can do is

Date

Dreams...

Wishes...

Phone Numbers...

Date ___

Today I am ___

Because ___

I wish I could ___

What I can do is ___

Date

Today I am

Because

I wish I could

What I can do is

Date

Today I am
_____
_____

Because
_____
_____
_____
_____
_____

I wish I could
_____
_____
_____
_____
_____
_____
_____

What I can do is
_____
_____
_____
_____
_____
_____
_____
_____

Date

What I said...

What I wish I had said...

Date

Today I am

Because

I wish I could

What I can do is

Date

Today I am

_____

_____

Because

_____

_____

_____

_____

I wish I could

_____

_____

_____

_____

_____

What I can do is

_____

_____

_____

_____

_____

_____

_____

 Today I am
_____
_____

Because
_____
_____
_____
_____

I wish I could
_____
_____
_____
_____
_____
_____

What I can do is
_____
_____
_____
_____
_____
_____
_____

Date

Today I am

_____
_____
_____

Because

_____
_____
_____
_____
_____

I wish I could

What I can do is

Date

Today I am

_____
_____

Because

_____
_____
_____
_____
_____

I wish I could

_____
_____
_____
_____
_____
_____
_____

What I can do is

_____
_____
_____
_____
_____
_____
_____

Date

Date

Today I am
_____
_____

Because
_____
_____
_____
_____

I wish I could
_____
_____
_____
_____
_____

What I can do is
_____
_____
_____
_____
_____
_____

Date

Today I am

_____

_____

Because

_____

_____

_____

_____

I wish I could

_____

_____

_____

_____

_____

_____

What I can do is

_____

_____

_____

_____

_____

_____

_____

Date

Today I am

___

___

Because

___

___

___

___

I wish I could

___

___

___

___

___

What I can do is

___

___

___

___

___

___

___

Date

Today I am
_____
_____

Because
_____
_____
_____
_____

I wish I could
_____
_____
_____
_____
_____
_____

What I can do is
_____
_____
_____
_____
_____
_____
_____

Date

Today I am

___

Because

___

I wish I could

___

What I can do is

___

Date

#@!@#$

Words I use when I'm Angry	...when I'm really angry	Words I could use instead
1.	1.	1.
2.	2.	2.
3.	3.	3.
4.	4.	4.
5.	5.	5.
6.	6.	6.
7.	7.	7.
8.	8.	8.
9.	9.	9.
10.	10.	10.
11.	11.	11.
12.	12.	12.
13.	13.	13.
14.	14.	14.
15.	15.	15.

Date

Today I am

Because

I wish I could

What I can do is

Date

Today I am

_____
_____

Because

_____
_____
_____
_____

I wish I could

_____
_____
_____
_____
_____

What I can do is

_____
_____
_____
_____
_____
_____

Date

Today I am
_____
_____

Because
_____
_____
_____
_____

I wish I could
_____
_____
_____
_____
_____
_____

What I can do is
_____
_____
_____
_____
_____
_____
_____

Date

Today I am
_____
_____

Because
_____
_____
_____
_____
_____

I wish I could
_____
_____
_____
_____
_____
_____

What I can do is
_____
_____
_____
_____
_____
_____
_____

Date

Today I am

Because

I wish I could

What I can do is

Date

Try This

Combine at least 1 word from column 1, at least 1 word from column 2, and only 1 word from column 3 for epic results.

What I came up with

Column 1	Column 2	Column 3
artless	awful	apple-john
bawdy	base-court	basket-cockle
beslubbering	bat-fowling	baggage
bootless	beef-witted	barnacle
caluminous	beetle-headed	bladder
churlish	boil-brained	blind-worm
clouted	brazen-faced	boar-pig
cockered	bunch-back'd	bugbear
craven	burly-boned	bum-bailey
cullionly	clapper-clawed	canker-blossom
currish	clay-brained	clack-dish
dankish	common-kissing	clotpole
dissembling	crook-pated	codpiece
droning	dismal-dreaming	coxcomb
errant	dizzy-eyed	death-token
fawning	doghearted	devil-monk
fobbing	dread-bolted	dewberry
frothy	earth-vexing	flap-dragon
froward	elf-skinned	flax-wench

_____

_____

_____

_____

_____

_____

_____

_____

Today I am
_____
_____

Because
_____
_____
_____
_____
_____

I wish I could
_____
_____
_____
_____
_____
_____
_____

What I can do is
_____
_____
_____
_____
_____
_____
_____
_____

Date

Today I am

_____

_____

Because

_____

_____

_____

_____

I wish I could

_____

_____

_____

_____

_____

What I can do is

_____

_____

_____

_____

_____

_____

_____

Date

Today I am

_____
_____

Because

_____
_____
_____
_____

I wish I could

_____
_____
_____
_____
_____

What I can do is

_____
_____
_____
_____
_____
_____

Date

Thoughts...

Ideas...

Random Doodles...

Date

Today I am

_____
_____
_____

Because

_____
_____
_____
_____
_____

I wish I could

_____
_____
_____
_____
_____
_____

What I can do is

_____
_____
_____
_____
_____
_____
_____

Date

Today I am

_____
_____
_____

Because

_____
_____
_____
_____
_____

I wish I could

_____
_____
_____
_____
_____
_____

What I can do is

_____
_____
_____
_____
_____
_____
_____

Date

Date

Today I am
_____
_____

Because
_____
_____
_____
_____

I wish I could
_____
_____
_____
_____
_____

What I can do is
_____
_____
_____
_____
_____
_____
_____

Date

Today I am

___

Because

___

I wish I could

___

What I can do is

___

Date

Today I am

_____
_____
_____

Because

_____
_____
_____
_____
_____

I wish I could

_____
_____
_____
_____
_____
_____

What I can do is

_____
_____
_____
_____
_____
_____
_____

Date

Today I am

___

Because

___

I wish I could

___

What I can do is

___

Date

Today I am

Because

I wish I could

What I can do is

Date

Today I am
_____
_____

Because
_____
_____
_____
_____

I wish I could
_____
_____
_____
_____
_____

What I can do is
_____
_____
_____
_____
_____
_____

Date

Say what you really mean

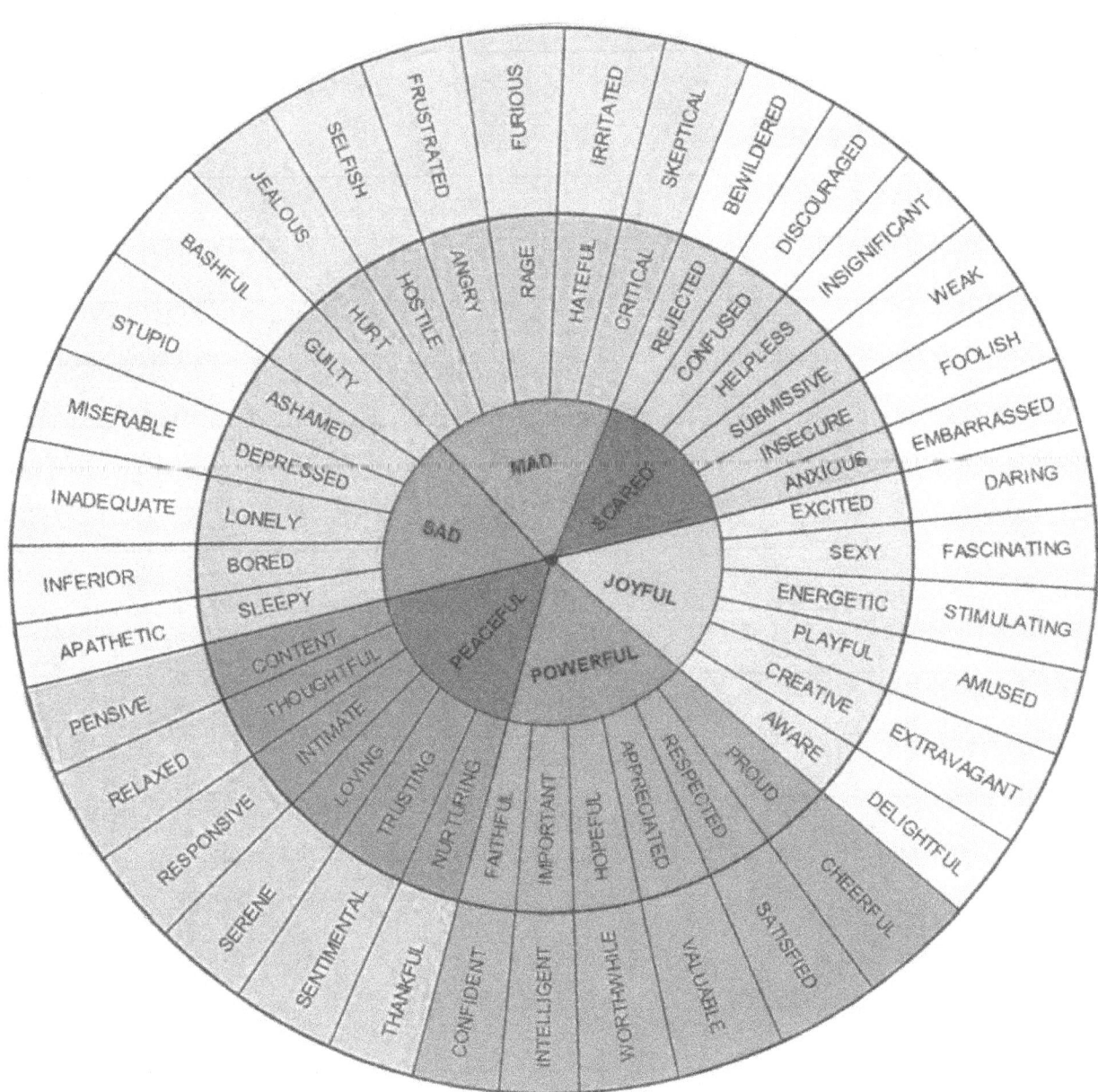

Date

Stuff...

Date

Today I am

_____
_____
_____

Because

_____
_____
_____
_____
_____

I wish I could

_____
_____
_____
_____
_____
_____

What I can do is

_____
_____
_____
_____
_____
_____
_____

Date

Today I am

_____
_____

Because

_____
_____
_____
_____

I wish I could

_____
_____
_____
_____
_____

What I can do is

_____
_____
_____
_____
_____
_____

Date

Today I am
_____
_____

Because
_____
_____
_____
_____

I wish I could
_____
_____
_____
_____
_____

What I can do is
_____
_____
_____
_____
_____
_____

Date

Today I am

Because

I wish I could

What I can do is

Date

Today I am

_____
_____
_____

Because

_____
_____
_____
_____
_____

I wish I could

_____
_____
_____
_____
_____

What I can do is

_____
_____
_____
_____
_____
_____

Date

Something that happened today

How I wish it happened

Date

Today I am

_____
_____
_____

Because

_____
_____
_____
_____
_____

I wish I could

_____
_____
_____
_____
_____
_____

What I can do is

_____
_____
_____
_____
_____
_____
_____

Date

Today I am

_____
_____

Because

_____
_____
_____
_____

I wish I could

_____
_____
_____
_____
_____

What I can do is

_____
_____
_____
_____
_____
_____

Date

Today I am
_____
_____

Because
_____
_____
_____
_____

I wish I could
_____
_____
_____
_____
_____

What I can do is
_____
_____
_____
_____
_____
_____

Date

Today I am

_____
_____
_____

Because

_____
_____
_____
_____
_____

I wish I could

_____
_____
_____
_____
_____
_____
_____

What I can do is

_____
_____
_____
_____
_____
_____
_____

Date

Today I am

Because

I wish I could

What I can do is

Date

Date

Try This

Combine at least 1 word from column 1, at least 1 word from column 2, and only 1 word from column 3 for epic results.

What I came up with

Column 1	Column 2	Column 3
gleeking	fen-sucked	foot-licker
goatish	fishified	fustilarian
gorbellied	flap-mouthed	giglet
impertinent	fly-bitten	gudgeon
infectious	folly-fallen	hag
jarring	fool-born	harpy
lily-livered	full-gorged	hedge-pig
loggerheaded	guts-griping	horn-beast
lumpish	half-faced	hugger-mugger
malmsey-nosed	hasty-witted	joithead
mammering	hedge-born	jolt-head
mangled	hell-hated	knave
mewling	idle-headed	lewdster
paunchy	ill-breeding	lout
pigeon-liver'd	ill-nurtured	maggot-pie
pribbling	knotty-pated	malcontent
puking	leering	malt-worm
puny	malcontented	mammet
qualling	milk-livered	measle

_____

_____

_____

_____

_____

_____

_____

_____

_____

Date

Today I am

_____
_____
_____

Because

_____
_____
_____
_____
_____

I wish I could

_____
_____
_____
_____
_____
_____

What I can do is

_____
_____
_____
_____
_____
_____
_____

Date

Today I am

_____
_____
_____

Because

_____
_____
_____
_____
_____

I wish I could

_____
_____
_____
_____
_____
_____

What I can do is

_____
_____
_____
_____
_____
_____
_____

Date

Today I am

___

___

Because

___

___

___

___

I wish I could

___

___

___

___

___

What I can do is

___

___

___

___

___

Date

Today I am

_____

_____

_____

Because

_____

_____

_____

_____

_____

I wish I could

_____

_____

_____

_____

_____

_____

What I can do is

_____

_____

_____

_____

_____

_____

_____

Date

Today I am
_____
_____
_____

Because
_____
_____
_____
_____
_____

I wish I could
_____
_____
_____
_____
_____
_____

What I can do is
_____
_____
_____
_____
_____
_____
_____

Date

Date

Date

Today I am

Because

I wish I could

What I can do is

Date

Today I am

_____
_____

Because

_____
_____
_____
_____

I wish I could

_____
_____
_____
_____
_____
_____

What I can do is

_____
_____
_____
_____
_____
_____
_____

Date

Today I am

_____
_____

Because

_____
_____
_____
_____

I wish I could

_____
_____
_____
_____

What I can do is

_____
_____
_____
_____
_____
_____

Date

Today I am

_____
_____
_____

Because

_____
_____
_____
_____
_____

I wish I could

_____
_____
_____
_____
_____
_____

What I can do is

_____
_____
_____
_____
_____
_____
_____

Date

Today I am
_____
_____
_____

Because
_____
_____
_____
_____
_____

I wish I could
_____
_____
_____
_____
_____
_____
_____

What I can do is
_____
_____
_____
_____
_____
_____
_____

Date

Try This

Combine at least 1 word from column 1, at least 1 word from column 2, and only 1 word from column 3 for epic results.

What I came up with

Column 1	Column 2	Column 3
rampallian	misbegotten	minnow
rank	motley-minded	miscreant
reeky	narcissistic	moldwarp
roguish	odiferous	muddy-mettled
ruttish	onion-eyed	mumble-news
saucy	plume-plucked	neophyte
scale-sided	poisonous	nut-hook
spleeny	pottle-deep	pigeon-egg
spongy	pox-marked	pignut
surly	reeling-ripe	popinjay
toad-spotted	rough-hewn	pumpion
tottering	rude-growing	puttock
unmuzzled	rump-fed	rascal
vain	scurvy-valiant	ratsbane
venomed	shard-borne	scullian
villainous	sheep-biting	scut
warped	spur-galled	skainsmate

_____

_____

_____

_____

_____

_____

_____

_____

Date

Today I am

___

Because

___

I wish I could

___

What I can do is

___

Date

Today I am

_____
_____
_____

Because

_____
_____
_____
_____
_____

I wish I could

_____
_____
_____
_____
_____
_____

What I can do is

_____
_____
_____
_____
_____
_____
_____

Date

Today I am

_____
_____
_____

Because

_____
_____
_____
_____

I wish I could

_____
_____
_____
_____
_____

What I can do is

_____
_____
_____
_____
_____
_____

Date

Today I am
_____
_____

Because
_____
_____
_____
_____

I wish I could
_____
_____
_____
_____
_____

What I can do is
_____
_____
_____
_____
_____
_____

Date

Today I am

_____
_____
_____

Because

_____
_____
_____
_____
_____

I wish I could

_____
_____
_____
_____
_____
_____

What I can do is

_____
_____
_____
_____
_____
_____
_____

Date

Something that happened today

How I wish it happened

Date

Today I am
_____
_____

Because
_____
_____
_____
_____

I wish I could
_____
_____
_____
_____
_____

What I can do is
_____
_____
_____
_____
_____
_____

Date

Today I am

Because

I wish I could

What I can do is

Date

Today I am
_____
_____
_____

Because
_____
_____
_____
_____

I wish I could
_____
_____
_____
_____
_____

What I can do is
_____
_____
_____
_____
_____
_____

Date

Today I am
_____
_____
_____

Because
_____
_____
_____
_____
_____

I wish I could
_____
_____
_____
_____
_____
_____

What I can do is
_____
_____
_____
_____
_____
_____
_____

Date

Today I am

___

Because

___

I wish I could

___

What I can do is

___

Date

Reasons to roll my eyes

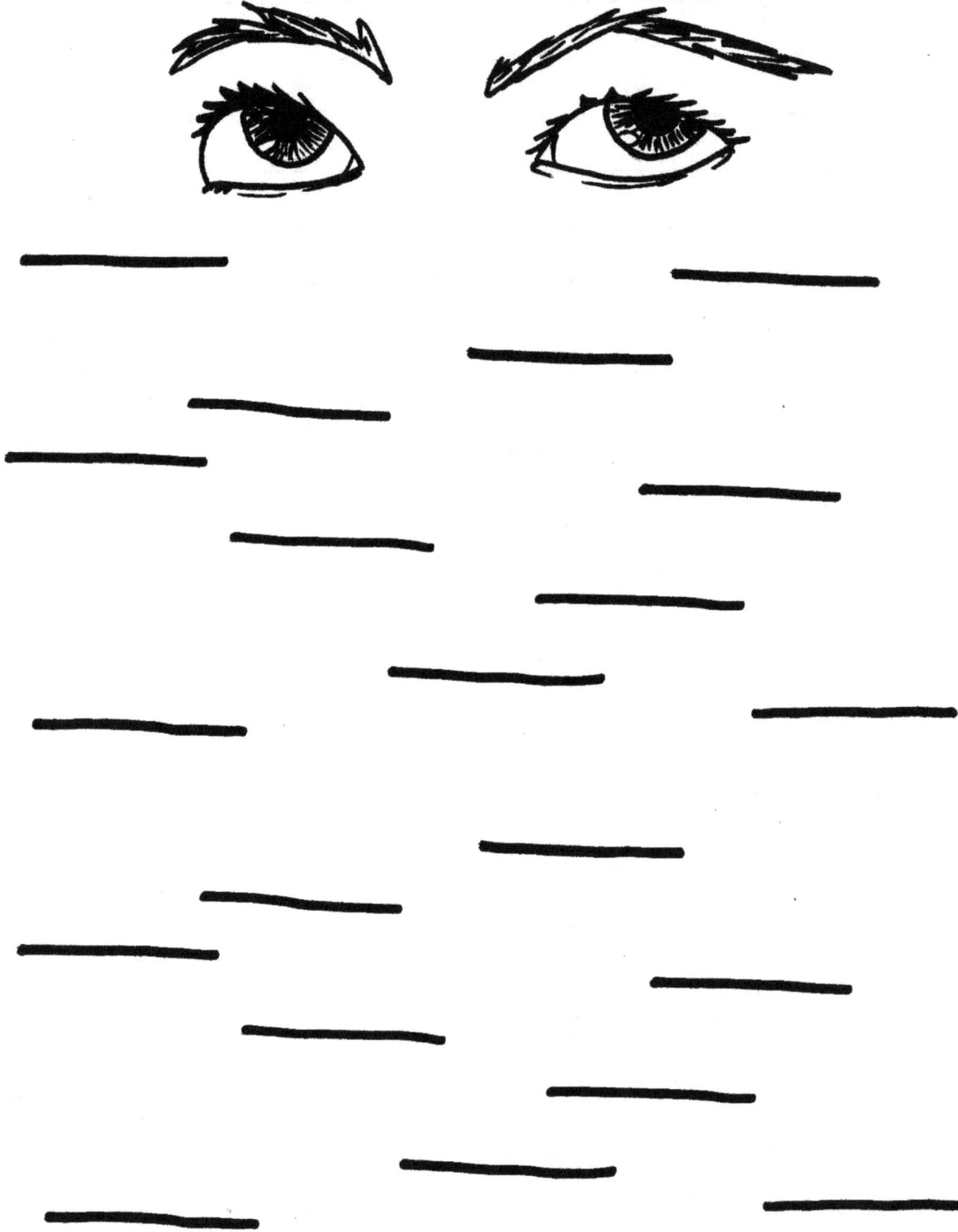

Date

Today I am
_____
_____

Because
_____
_____
_____
_____

I wish I could
_____
_____
_____
_____
_____

What I can do is
_____
_____
_____
_____
_____
_____

Date

Today I am

Because

I wish I could

What I can do is

Date

Today I am

Because

I wish I could

What I can do is

Date

Today I am

_____
_____
_____

Because

_____
_____
_____
_____
_____

I wish I could

_____
_____
_____
_____
_____
_____

What I can do is

_____
_____
_____
_____
_____
_____
_____

Date

Today I am
_____
_____

Because
_____
_____
_____
_____

I wish I could
_____
_____
_____
_____
_____
_____

What I can do is
_____
_____
_____
_____
_____
_____

Date

Try This

Combine at least 1 word from column 1, at least 1 word from column 2, and only 1 word from column 3 for epic results.

What I came up with

Column 1	Column 2	Column 3
decrepit	decaying	dewberry
despicable	deplorable	bit o baggage
dreadful	double-crossing	bladder
duplicitous	droning	blind-worm
fiendish	full-gorged	clot-pole
gibbering	ill-breeding	curmudgeon
horrendous	miserable	deadwood
lumpish	nefarious	death token
mangled	noxious	derelict
misbegotten	obsequious	dipwit
obtuse	pernicious	knave
petulant	pox-ridden	malcontent
putrid	putrid	miscreant
rank	repugnant	nut-hook
repugnant	scurvy-excreting	parasite
shoddy	scurvy-valiant	popinjay
snot-nosed	self-absorbed	sea-slug

_____

_____

_____

_____

_____

_____

_____

Date

Today I am

_____
_____

Because

_____
_____
_____
_____

I wish I could

_____
_____
_____
_____
_____

What I can do is

_____
_____
_____
_____
_____
_____

Date

Today I am
_____
_____
_____

Because
_____
_____
_____
_____
_____

I wish I could
_____
_____
_____
_____
_____

What I can do is
_____
_____
_____
_____
_____
_____

Date

Today I am

_____
_____
_____

Because

_____
_____
_____
_____
_____
_____

I wish I could

```
┌─────────────────────────────────────────────────┐
│                                                 │
│                                                 │
│                                                 │
│                                                 │
│                                                 │
└─────────────────────────────────────────────────┘
```

What I can do is

```
┌─────────────────────────────────────────────────┐
│                                                 │
│                                                 │
│                                                 │
│                                                 │
│                                                 │
└─────────────────────────────────────────────────┘
```

Date

Today I am

_____
_____
_____

Because

_____
_____
_____
_____
_____

I wish I could

_____
_____
_____
_____
_____
_____

What I can do is

_____
_____
_____
_____
_____
_____
_____

Date

Today I am

_____
_____

Because

_____
_____
_____
_____

I wish I could

_____
_____
_____
_____

What I can do is

_____
_____
_____
_____
_____
_____

Date

What I said...

What I meant...

Now what?

Date

Today I am
_____
_____
_____

Because
_____
_____
_____
_____
_____

I wish I could
_____
_____
_____
_____
_____

What I can do is
_____
_____
_____
_____
_____

Date
_____
_____

Today I am
_____
_____
_____

Because
_____
_____
_____
_____

I wish I could
_____
_____
_____
_____

What I can do is
_____
_____
_____
_____
_____

Date

Today I am

Because

I wish I could

What I can do is

Date
_____

Today I am
_____
_____

Because
_____
_____
_____
_____

I wish I could
_____
_____
_____
_____
_____

What I can do is
_____
_____
_____
_____
_____

Date

Today I am

Because

I wish I could

What I can do is

Date

Try This

Combine at least 1 word from column 1, at least 1 word from column 2, and only 1 word from column 3 for epic results.

What I came up with

column 1	column 2	column 3
beslubbering	beef-witted	bit o baggage
churlish	clay-brained	codpiece
coldblooded	covetous	cozener
creepy	crusty	curmudgeon
deceiving	degenerate	derelict
dreadful	double-crossing	dipwit
duplicitous	droning	dissembler
fawning	foul-mouthed	fiend
foul	full-gorged	flesh monger
heinous	hook-nosed	instigator
incontinent	ill-tempered	miscreant
insolent	shrill-tongued	trouser stain
wayward	tardy-gaited	vassal
weather-bitten	tickle-brained	villiago
weedy	unchin-snouted	wagtail
wimpled	unwash'd	wharf rat
yeasty	wretched	whey-face

_____

_____

_____

_____

_____

_____

_____

_____

Date

Today I am

_____
_____

Because

_____
_____
_____
_____

I wish I could

_____
_____
_____
_____
_____

What I can do is

_____
_____
_____
_____
_____
_____

Date

Today I am

_____
_____
_____

Because

_____
_____
_____
_____
_____

I wish I could

_____
_____
_____
_____
_____

What I can do is

_____
_____
_____
_____
_____
_____

Date

Today I am
_____
_____
_____

Because
_____
_____
_____
_____
_____

I wish I could
_____
_____
_____
_____
_____
_____
_____

What I can do is
_____
_____
_____
_____
_____
_____
_____

Date

Today I am

_____
_____
_____

Because

_____
_____
_____
_____
_____

I wish I could

_____
_____
_____
_____
_____
_____

What I can do is

_____
_____
_____
_____
_____
_____
_____

Date

Today I am
_____
_____
_____

Because
_____
_____
_____
_____
_____

I wish I could
_____
_____
_____
_____
_____
_____

What I can do is
_____
_____
_____
_____
_____
_____
_____

Date

Date

Today I am
_____
_____
_____

Because
_____
_____
_____
_____
_____

I wish I could
_____
_____
_____
_____
_____
_____

What I can do is
_____
_____
_____
_____
_____
_____
_____

Date

Today I am

_____
_____
_____

Because

_____
_____
_____
_____
_____

I wish I could

_____
_____
_____
_____
_____
_____

What I can do is

_____
_____
_____
_____
_____
_____
_____

Date

Today I am

_____
_____
_____

Because

_____
_____
_____
_____
_____

I wish I could

_____
_____
_____
_____
_____
_____

What I can do is

_____
_____
_____
_____
_____
_____
_____

Date

Today I am

_____

_____

_____

Because

_____

_____

_____

_____

_____

I wish I could

_____

_____

_____

_____

_____

_____

What I can do is

_____

_____

_____

_____

_____

_____

_____

Date

Today I am
_____
_____

Because
_____
_____
_____
_____

I wish I could
_____
_____
_____
_____
_____

What I can do is
_____
_____
_____
_____
_____
_____

Date

So this happened...

About The Author

Dana Kirk has been teaching and working with teens since 2006. Her school year typically doesn't start until somebody throws a desk. She has seen lots of angry kids who have been given a list of "NOPEs" as long as a bus. When Dana gets angry, she writes. Sometimes she writes dialogue or fight scenes for her novels. Sometimes she makes up pirate curses. To help her students she could have written all of the ways it is not okay to express your anger. Instead, she made one place to put those angry thoughts.

www.ingramcontent.com/pod-product-compliance
Lightning Source LLC
Chambersburg PA
CBHW081014040426
42444CB00014B/3207